Wisdom for MEN

Practical Bible-based Principles
for Home and Work

BOBB BIEHL

JOURNEY
OOKS

D071147:

WISDOM FOR MEN
Copyright © 1994 by Bobb Biehl

Published by LifeJourney Books, an imprint of Chariot Family Publishing
a division of David C. Cook Publishing Co.
David C. Cook Publishing Co., Elgin, Illinois
David C. Cook Publishing Co., Weston, Ontario
Nova Distribution Ltd., Newton Abbot, England

Scripture quotations are from the following translations:
KJV: Holy Bible Authorized King James Version
NCV: New Century Version, copyright © 1991 by Word Publishing, Dallas, Texas 75039.
    Used by permission.
NEB: The New English Bible, copyright © 1961/1970 by The Delegates of the Oxford
    University Press and The Syndics of the Cambridge University Press
NIV: Holy Bible, New International Version. Copyright © 1973, 1978, 1984 by International
    Bible Society. Used by permission of Zondervan Publishing House. All rights reserved.
NKJV: New King James Version. Copyright © 1979, 1980, 1982, Thomas Nelson, Inc.
Phillips: The New Testament in Modern English, Revised Edition, copyright © 1958, 1960,
    1972 by J. B. Phillips, copyright © 1955 *Letters to Young Churches* by The Macmillan
    Company.
TLB: The Living Bible © 1971. Used by permission of Tyndale House Publishers, Inc.,
    Wheaton, IL 60189. All rights reserved.

First Printing, 1994   Printed in the United States of America
98 97 96 95 94   5 4 3 2 1

My father, Robert Lee Biehl, has spent over fifty years sharing with me his Nutshells (bits of practical wisdom). He has modeled for me an integration of both scriptural and day-to-day wisdom.

My father-in-law, Joseph Henry Kimbel, has been just as generous with his Pastor's Heart Wisdom since I first began dating his daughter, Cheryl Ann, at the "greenhorn" age of twenty-one.

My son, J. Ira Biehl, also teaches me as I observe his street wisdom and common sense. I grow personally as he explains his concepts like Refined Skills.

I would like to dedicate this book to these three great men in my life.

Bobb Biehl

INTRODUCTION

"Blessed is the man who finds wisdom," said Solomon. This has a warm and significant sound, but just what does it mean in our generation thousands and thousands of years after it was written?

Try asking a few close friends, "What makes a person wise?" Do not be surprised if you get a few "foggy" answers. You would likely get very clear answers to questions like: what makes a person strong? What makes one popular? What makes a person sexy?

Today few have a good definition for "wise" or any idea about how to become wise. Even after studying the subject of wisdom for years, I still find it far easier to explain wisdom than to define it.

I am convinced that people who have wisdom are those who have the ability to answer three questions:

What should I do next?

Why would you suggest that?

What resources should I bring to bear on this need?

The better you are at answering these questions, the wiser you will be.

But, you may ask, what is godly wisdom as compared to earthly wisdom? Godly wisdom is asking a slightly modified version of these three questions:

What would God do/advise next in this situation?
Why would He do/suggest that?
What resources would He bring to bear on this need?

This book is a collection of the most important life principles I have written and collected from a number of sources over the years. I offer them to you as food for thought, reflection, and serious prayer. As Solomon said, "Pay attention and listen to the saying of the wise; apply your heart to what I teach, for it is pleasing when you keep them in your heart and have all of them ready on your lips." (NIV)

MARRIAGE & FAMILY PRINCIPLES

Love people and use things.
Don't love things and
use people.

Art DeMoss

♦ What a [person] desires is unfailing love. PROVERBS 19:22 (NIV)

♦ No servant can be the slave of two masters; for either he will hate the first and love the second, or he will be devoted to the first and think nothing of the second. You cannot serve God and Money. MATTHEW 6:24 (NEB)

♦ Though I speak with the tongues of men and of angels, but have not love, I have become as sounding brass or a clanging cymbal. And though I have the gift of prophecy, and understand all mysteries and all knowledge, and though I have all faith, so that I could remove mountains, but have not love, I am nothing. And though I bestow all my goods to feed the poor, and though I give my body to be burned, but have not love, it profits me nothing. 1 CORINTHIANS 13:1-3 (NKJV)

Nobody wants to fail.
People most often fail because
they just don't know how
to succeed.

♦ Plans fail without good advice, but plans succeed with the advice from many others. PROVERBS 15:22 (NCV)

People need encouragement
and instruction more
than criticism.

♦ We beg you, brothers, to acknowledge those who are working so hard among you, and in the Lord's fellowship are your leaders and counsellors. Hold them in the highest possible esteem and affection for the work they do. You must live at peace among yourselves. And we would urge you, brothers, to admonish the careless, encourage the faint-hearted, support the weak, and to be very patient with them all. 1 THESSALONIANS 5:12-14 (NEB)

Unity is the result of diversity … not uniformity. What if everyone on the team wanted to be quarterback?

♦ I appeal to you, brothers, in the name of our Lord Jesus Christ, that all of you agree with one another so that there may be no divisions among you and that you may be perfectly united in mind and thought. 1 CORINTHIANS 1:10 (NIV)

Remember that more marriages end as a result of disagreements about money than any other reason.

♦ Better a little with the fear of the Lord than great wealth with turmoil. Better a meal of vegetables where there is love than a fattened calf with hatred.
PROVERBS 15:16-17 (NIV)

♦ We brought nothing into the world, so we can take nothing out. But if we have food and clothes, we will be satisfied with that. Those who want to become rich bring temptation to themselves and are caught in a trap. They want many foolish and harmful things that ruin and destroy people. The love of money causes all kinds of evil. Some people have left the faith, because they wanted to get more money, but they have caused themselves much sorrow.
1 TIMOTHY 6:7-10 (NCV)

Don't overlook old people. Here is wisdom and experience for our asking. Here, also, is a group to whom we must give kindness and affection.

Dr. John R. Mott

♦ Rise in the presence of the aged, show respect for the elderly and revere your God. I am the Lord. LEVITICUS 19:32 (NIV)

Encouragement brings hope for the future. Specialize in being an encourager.

♦ Learn to do right! Seek justice, encourage the oppressed. Defend the cause of the fatherless, plead the case of the widow. ISAIAH 1:17 (NIV)

♦ We have different gifts, according to the grace given us. If a man's gift is prophesying, let him use it in proportion to his faith. If it is serving, let him serve; if it is teaching, let him teach; if it is encouraging, let him encourage; if it is contributing to the needs of others, let him give generously; if it is leadership, let him govern diligently; if it is showing mercy, let him do it cheerfully. ROMANS 12:6-8 (NIV)

♦ But let us who live in the light keep sober, protected by the armor of faith and love, and wearing as our helmet the happy hope of salvation. For God has not chosen to pour out his anger upon us, but to save us through our Lord Jesus Christ; he died for us so that we can live with him forever, whether we are dead or alive at the time of his return. So encourage each other to build each other up, just as you are already doing. 1 THESSALONIANS 5:8-11 (TLB)

FINANCIAL PRINCIPLES

In your early years of making money, live as frugally as possible in order that you may invest as much as possible.

Dr. R. C. Sproul

◆ Go to the ant, you sluggard; consider its ways and be wise! It has no commander, no overseer or ruler, yet it stores its provisions in summer and gathers its food at harvest. PROVERBS 6:6-8 (NIV)

◆ Keep your lives free from the love of money and be content with what you have, because God has said, "Never will I leave you; never will I forsake you." HEBREWS 13:5 (NIV)

When investing money,
seek advice from those who have
expertise in the area of your
investment. Pay generously for that
counsel. Scrutinize carefully advice
from those who are selling.

Lee Eaton

♦ Listen to advice and accept instruction, and you will die a wise man.
PROVERBS 19:20 (NEB)

♦ Make plans by seeking advice. PROVERBS 20:18 (NIV)

Know what it costs to live, and live within your means.

Dennis R. James

♦ Let your conduct be without covetousness, and be content with such things as you have. For He Himself has said, "I will never leave you nor forsake you." HEBREWS 13:5 (NKJV)

Borrow only for things that will increase in value.

Dr. Robert C. Andringa

♦ Let no debt remain outstanding, except the continuing debt to love one another, for he who loves his fellowman has fulfilled the law. ROMANS 13:8 (NIV)

"You can't win 'em all."
You will have financial setbacks
and disappointment, but ... this
phrase will help you over the
rough places of your life.

Robert L. Biehl (my father)

◆ When life is good, enjoy it. But when life is hard, remember: God gives us good times and hard times, and no one knows what tomorrow will bring.
ECCLESIASTES 7:14 (NCV)

◆ We are hard pressed on every side, but not crushed; perplexed, but not in despair; persecuted, but not abandoned; struck down, but not destroyed.
2 CORINTHIANS 4:8, 9 (NIV)

Don't spend money you don't have.

◆ You shall not covet your neighbor's house; you shall not covet your neighbor's wife, nor his manservant, nor his maidservant, nor his ox, nor his donkey, nor anything that is your neighbor's. EXODUS 20:17 (NKJV)

◆ But godliness with contentment is great gain. 1 TIMOTHY 6:6 (KJV)

People who make money extremely fast usually lose it or spend it all. People who make money over a longer period of time tend to keep it.

David M. Harmon

◆ Lazy hands make a man poor, but diligent hands bring wealth. PROVERBS 10:4 (NIV)

Making money requires motivation. Determine early what you want to use money for, and make that your goal. Never make your goal just money.

Joe Kimbel

♦ The sluggard craves and gets nothing, but the desires of the diligent are fully satisfied. PROVERBS 13:4 (NIV)

Investigate and gather as much information about an investment as possible.

Timothy S. Sambrano

♦ Every prudent man acts out of knowledge, but a fool exposes his folly.
PROVERBS 13:16 (NIV)

Hold all you have with a loose grip.

Mark Petersburg

♦ You suffered with those thrown into jail, and you were actually joyful when all you owned was taken from you, knowing that better things were awaiting you in heaven, things that would be yours forever. Do not let this happy trust in the Lord die away, no matter what happens. Remember your reward!
HEBREWS 10:34, 35 (TLB)

When you are thinking of making any investment, take twenty-four hours to "sleep on it." Think about the investment nonemotionally.

Robert D. Smullin

♦ It is a trap for a man to dedicate something rashly and only later to consider his vows. PROVERBS 20:25 (NIV)

Risk only what you can afford to lose.

R. Michael Carter

♦ A stranger…asked, "Good Master, what must I do to win eternal life?" Jesus said to him, "…You know the commandments…." "But, Master," he replied, "I have kept all these since I was a boy."… His heart warmed to him, and he said, "One thing you lack: go, sell everything you have, and give to the poor, and you will have riches in heaven; and come, follow me." At these words his face fell and he went away with a heavy heart; for he was a man of great wealth.
MARK 10:17-22 (NEB)

Start saving money now. People think in order to save a lot of money, you have to make a lot of money. In reality, acquiring a substantial sum of money requires only two things: time and the discipline to consistently work toward a goal.

Jack Hanslik

♦ Dishonest money dwindles away, but he who gathers money little by little makes it grow. PROVERBS 13:11 (NIV)

Your teachability will remain one of the bedrock issues for you to make the most of … making money, and then in the management of that money after you have it.

Dennis Raney

♦ Wisdom and good judgment live together, for wisdom knows where to discover knowledge and understanding. If anyone respects and fears God, he will hate evil. For wisdom hates pride, arrogance, corruption and deceit of every kind. "I, Wisdom, give good advice and common sense. Because of my strength, kings reign in power. I show the judges who is right and who is wrong. Rulers rule well with my help. I love all who love me. Those who search for me shall surely find me. Unending riches, honor, justice and righteousness are mine to distribute. My gifts are better than the purest gold or sterling silver! My paths are those of justice and right. Those who love and follow me are indeed wealthy. I fill their treasuries." PROVERBS 8:12-21 (TLB)

PRACTICAL BIBLE-BASED PRINCIPLES · FOR HOME AND WORK ·

PERSONAL PRINCIPLES

If you can't trust a person
at all points, you can't truly
trust him or her at any point.

Cheryl Biehl

♦ Truthful lips endure forever, but a lying tongue lasts only a moment.
PROVERBS 12:19 (NIV)

♦ Again, the law of Moses says, "You shall not break your vows to God, but must fulfill them all." But I say: Don't make any vows! And even to say, "By heavens!" is a sacred vow to God, for the heavens are God's throne. And if you say "By the earth!" it is a sacred vow, for the earth is his footstool. And don't swear "By Jerusalem!" for Jerusalem is the capital of the great King. Don't even swear "By my head!" for you can't turn one hair white or black. Say just a simple "Yes, I will" or "No, I won't." Your word is enough. To strengthen your promise with a vow shows that something is wrong. MATTHEW 5:33-37 (TLB)

Deal with circumstances as they are, not as you wish they were.

♦ And we know that all things work together for good to those who love God, to those who are the called according to His purpose. For whom He foreknew, He also predestined to be conformed to the image of his Son, that He might be the firstborn among many brethren. Moreover whom He predestined, these He also called; whom He called, these He also justified; and whom He justified, these He also glorified. What then shall we say to these things? If God is for us, who can be against us? ROMANS 8:28-31 (NKJV)

♦ Be joyful always; pray continually; give thanks in all circumstances, for this is God's will for you in Christ Jesus. 1 THESSALONIANS 5:16-18 (NIV)

Successful people work harder than the others.

Bo Mitchell

♦ Diligence brings a man to power, but laziness to forced labour. PROVERBS 12:24 (NEB)

♦ All hard work brings a profit, but mere talk leads only to poverty. PROVERBS 14:23 (NIV)

You can't have it all. You don't want it all.

♦ I searched in my heart how to gratify my flesh with wine, while guiding my heart with wisdom, and how to lay hold on folly, till I might see what was good for the sons of men to do under heaven all the days of their lives. I made my works great, I built myself houses, and planted myself vineyards. I made myself gardens and orchards, and I planted all kinds of fruit trees in them. I made myself waterpools from which to water the growing trees of the grove. I acquired male and female servants, and had servants born in my house. Yes, I had greater possessions of herds and flocks than all who were in Jerusalem before me. I also gathered for myself silver and gold and the special treasures of kings and of the provinces. I acquired male and female singers, the delights of the sons of men, and musical instruments of all kinds. So I became great and excelled more than all who were before me in Jerusalem. Also my wisdom remained with me. Whatever my eyes desired I did not keep from them. I did not withhold my heart from any pleasure. For my heart rejoiced in all my labor; And this was my reward from all my labor. Then I looked on all the works that my hands had done And on the labor in which I had toiled; And indeed all was vanity and grasping for the wind. There was no profit under the sun. ECCLESIASTES 2:3-11 (NKJV)

Think and speak for yourself.

♦ What do you think? If a man owns a hundred sheep, and one of them wanders away, will he not leave the ninety-nine on the hills and go to look for the one that wandered off? MATTHEW 18:12 (NIV)

♦ What do you think? There was a man who had two sons … MATTHEW 21:28 (NIV)

♦ What do you think about the Christ? Whose son is he? MATTHEW 22:42 (NIV)

♦ What do you think? MATTHEW 26:66 (NIV)

A mistake is only failure if you don't learn from it.

Dr. Roland Niednagel

♦ Flog a mocker, and the simple will learn prudence; rebuke a discerning man, and he will gain knowledge. PROVERBS 19:25 (NIV)

♦ Who can understand his errors? Cleanse me from secret faults. PSALM 19:12 (NKJV)

Life without goals is like a race without a finish line.

Ed Trenner

♦ My brothers, I do not consider myself to have grasped it fully even now. But I do concentrate on this: I forget all that lies behind me and with hands outstretched to whatever lies ahead I go straight for my goal—my reward the honour of my high calling by God in Christ Jesus. My ambition is the true goal of the spiritually adult: make it yours too. PHILIPPIANS 3:13-15 (PHILLIPS)

The first impression will be of your clothes. The lasting impression will be of your heart.

♦ Then the Lord said to Samuel, "How long will you mourn for Saul, seeing I have rejected him from reigning over Israel? Fill your horn with oil, and go; I am sending you to Jesse the Bethlehemite. For I have provided Myself a king among his sons." So it was, when they came, that he looked at Eliab and said, "Surely the Lord's anointed is before Him." But the Lord said to Samuel, "Do not look at his appearance or at the height of his stature, because I have refused him. For the Lord does not see as man sees; for man looks at the outward appearance, but the Lord looks at the heart." 1 SAMUEL 16:1, 6, 7 (NKJV)

Listen to God. Listen to yourself. Listen to trusted family and friends. Ignore the crowd.

♦ The Lord said, "Go out and stand on the mountain in the presence of the Lord, for the Lord is about to pass by." Then a great and powerful wind tore the mountains apart and shattered the rocks before the Lord, but the Lord was not in the wind. After the wind there was an earthquake, but the Lord was not in the earthquake. After the earthquake came fire, but the Lord was not in the fire. And after the fire came a gentle whisper. 1 KINGS 19:11, 12 (NIV)

♦ My child, listen to your father's teaching, and do not forget your mother's advice. Their teaching will be like flowers in your hair or a necklace around your neck. PROVERBS 1:8, 9 (NCV)

♦ Perfume and incense bring joy to the heart, and the pleasantness of one's friend springs from his earnest counsel. PROVERBS 27:9 (NIV)

♦ I beseech you therefore, brethren, by the mercies of God, that ye present your bodies a living sacrifice, holy, acceptable unto God, which is your reasonable service. And be not conformed to this world: but be ye transformed by the renewing of your mind, that ye may prove what is that good, and acceptable, and perfect will of God. ROMANS 12:1, 2 (KJV)

PHYSICAL PRINCIPLES

In sexual matters, trust your steering more than your brakes.

♦ Avoid sexual looseness like the plague! Every other sin that a man commits is done outside his own body, but this is an offence against his own body.
1 CORINTHIANS 6:18 (PHILLIPS)

Fatigue makes cowards of us all.

Vince Lombardi

♦ Have you not known? Have you not heard? The everlasting God, the Lord, the Creator of the ends of the earth, neither faints nor is weary. There is no searching of His understanding. He gives power to the weak, and to those who have no might He increases strength. Even the youths shall faint and be weary, and the young men shall utterly fall, but those who wait on the Lord shall renew their strength; they shall mount up with wings like eagles, they shall run and not be weary, they shall walk and not faint. ISAIAH 40:28-31 (NKJV)

Don't worry—be thankful.

♦ Do not worry about anything, but pray and ask God for everything you need, always giving thanks. PHILIPPIANS 4:6 (NCV)

Look people in the eye.

♦ A scoundrel, a mischievous man, is he who prowls about with crooked talk—a wink of the eye, a touch with the foot, a sign with the fingers. Subversion is the evil that he is plotting, he stirs up quarrels all the time.
PROVERBS 6:12-14 (NEB)

When you meet a person
who is different from you, or
someone whom others shun,
focus on the person and not
on that which differentiates.

♦ The Jewish leaders and Pharisees brought a woman caught in adultery and placed her out in front of the staring crowd. "Teacher," they said to Jesus, "this woman was caught in the very act of adultery. Moses' law says to kill her. What about it?" They were trying to trap him into saying something they could use against him, but Jesus stooped down and wrote in the dust with his finger. They kept demanding an answer, so he stood up again and said, "All right, hurl the stones at her until she dies. But only he who never sinned may throw the first!" Then he stooped down again and wrote some more in the dust. And the Jewish leaders slipped away one by one, beginning with the eldest, until only Jesus was left in front of the crowd with the woman. Then Jesus stood up again and said to her, "Where are your accusers? Didn't even one of them condemn you?" "No, sir," she said. And Jesus said, "Neither do I. Go and sin no more." JOHN 8:3-11 (TLB)

CAREER PRINCIPLES

Nothing is meaningful
without a context or
comparison.

The prophet proved this as he compared the incomparable God to idols:

♦ To whom will you compare me or count me equal? To whom will you liken me that we may be compared? Some pour out gold from their bags and weigh out silver on the scales; they hire a goldsmith to make it into a god, and they bow down and worship it. They lift it to their shoulders and carry it; they set it up in its place, and there it stands. From that spot it cannot move. Though one cries out to it, it does not answer; it cannot save him from his troubles. Remember this, fix it in mind, take it to heart, you rebels. Remember the former things, those of long ago; I am God, and there is no other; I am God, and there is none like me. ISAIAH 46:5-9 (NIV)

Leadership is knowing what to do next, knowing why that's important, and knowing how to bring the appropriate resources to bear on the need at hand.

♦ Now in those days, when the number of the disciples was multiplying, there arose a murmuring against the Hebrews by the Hellenists, because their widows were neglected in the daily distribution. Then the twelve summoned the multitude of the disciples and said, "It is not desirable that we should leave the word of God and serve tables. Therefore, brethren, seek out from among you seven men of good reputation, full of the Holy Spirit and wisdom, whom we may appoint over this business; but we will give ourselves continually to prayer and to the ministry of the word." And the saying pleased the whole multitude. And they chose Stephen, a man full of faith and the Holy Spirit and Philip, Prochorus, Nicanor, Timon, Parmenas, and Nicolas, a proselyte from Antioch, whom they set before the apostles; and when they had prayed, they laid hands on them. And the word of God spread, and the number of disciples multiplied greatly in Jerusalem, and a great many of the priests were obedient to the faith.
ACTS 6:1-7 (NKJV)

Deciding what not to do is just as important as deciding what to do.

Archie B. Parrish

♦ A Pharisee named Gamaliel, a teacher of the law, who was honored by all the people, stood up in the Sanhedrin and ordered that the men be put outside for a little while. Then he addressed them: "'Men of Israel, consider carefully what you intend to do to these men. Some time ago Theudas appeared, claiming to be somebody, and about four hundred men rallied to him. He was killed, all his followers were dispersed, and it all came to nothing. After him, Judas the Galilean appeared in the days of the census and led a band of people in revolt. He too was killed, and all his followers were scattered. Therefore, in the present case I advise you: Leave these men alone! Let them go! For if their purpose or activity is of human origin, it will fail. But if it is from God, you will not be able to stop these men; you will only find yourselves fighting against God."
ACTS 5:34-39 (NIV)

Invest your time wisely:
80% where you are strongest,
15% on learning new things,
and 5% where you need or
want to grow.

♦ Again, the Kingdom of Heaven can be illustrated by the story of a man going into another country, who called together his servants and loaned them money to invest for him while he was gone. He gave $5,000 to one, $2,000 to another, and $1,000 to the last—dividing it in proportion to their abilities—and then left on his trip. After a long time their master returned from his trip and called them to him to account for his money. The man to whom he had entrusted the $5,000 brought him $10,000. His master praised him for good work. Next came the man who had received the $2,000 with the report, "Sir, you gave me $2,000 to use, and I have doubled it." "Good work," his master said. "You are a good and faithful servant." Then the man with the $1,000 came and said, "Sir, I knew you were a hard man and I was afraid you would rob me of what I earned, so I hid your money in the earth and here it is!" But his master replied, "Wicked man! Lazy slave! Since you knew I would demand your profit, you should at least have put my money into the bank so I could have some interest. Take the money from this man and give it to the man with the $10,000. For the man who uses well what he is given shall be given more, and he shall have abundance. But from the man who is unfaithful, even what little responsibility he has shall be taken from him."

MATTHEW 25:14, 15, 19-21a, 22-23a, 24-29 (TLB)

An activity is work only
when you'd rather be doing
something else.

♦ So I commend the enjoyment of life, because nothing is better for a man under the sun than to eat and drink and be glad. Then joy will accompany him in his work all the days of the life God has given him under the sun.
ECCLESIASTES 8:15 (NIV)

Most of your business opportunities or career positions will be obtained through personal contacts. Now is the time for you to develop a personal network.

Loren Miller

♦ A good name is to be chosen rather than great riches, Loving favor rather than silver and gold. PROVERBS 22:1 (NKJV)

♦ A good name is better than fine perfume. ECCLESIASTES 7:1 (NIV)

Once the facts are clear, the decisions jump out at you.

Dr. Peter Drucker

♦ So Pilate, the governor, went out to them and asked, "What is your charge against this man? What are you accusing him of doing?"

"We wouldn't have arrested him if he weren't a criminal!" they retorted.

"Then take him away and judge him yourselves by your own laws," Pilate told them.

"But we want him crucified," they demanded, "and your approval is required."

Then Pilate went back into the palace and called for Jesus to be brought to him. "Are you the king of the Jews?" he asked him.

"'King' as you use the word or as the Jews use it?" Jesus asked.

"Am I a Jew?" Pilate retorted. "Your own people and their chief priests brought you here. Why? What have you done?"

Then Jesus answered, "I am not an earthly king. If I were, my followers would have fought when I was arrested by the Jewish leaders. But my Kingdom is not of the world." Pilate replied, "But you are a king then?"

"Yes," Jesus said. "I was born for that purpose. And I came to bring truth to the world. All who love the truth are my followers."

"What is truth?" Pilate exclaimed. Then he went out again to the people and told them, "He is not guilty of any crime." JOHN 18:29-31, 33-38 (TLB)

SOCIAL PRINCIPLES

To lose friends, brag about yourself. To gain friends, brag about others.

◆ Otherwise you will be bragging about your own plans, and such self-confidence never pleases God. JAMES 4:16 (TLB)

◆ If anyone is going to boast, let him boast about what the Lord has done and not about himself. 2 CORINTHIANS 10:17 (TLB)

◆ Don't be selfish; don't live to make a good impression on others. Be humble, thinking of others as better than yourself. PHILIPPIANS 2:3 (TLB)

Concentrate on caring, not just conversations.

♦ It is to freedom that you have been called, my brothers. Only be careful that freedom does not become mere opportunity for your lower nature. You should be free to serve each other in love. For after all, the whole Law toward others is summed up by this one command, "Thou shalt love thy neighbor as thyself." But if freedom means merely that you are free to attack and tear each other to pieces, be careful that it doesn't mean that between you you destroy your fellowship altogether! Here is my advice. Live your whole life in the Spirit and you will not satisfy the desires of your lower nature. GALATIANS 5:13-16 (PHILLIPS)

To make a good friend,
be a good friend.

♦ Do to others what you want them to do to you. LUKE 6:31 (NCV)

People do what makes sense
to them.

♦ The way of a fool seems right to him, but a wise man listens to advice.
PROVERBS 12:15 (NIV)

If you know how to ask a good question and then listen, you will never run out of good conversation.

♦ My dear brothers, take note of this: Everyone should be quick to listen, slow to speak.… JAMES 1:19 (NIV)

Make asking and collecting
questions a lifelong hobby.

♦ But, I ask… ROMANS 10:18 (NEB)

♦ But, I ask again… ROMANS 10:19 (NEB)

♦ I ask then… ROMANS 11:1 (NEB)

♦ I now ask… ROMANS 11:11 (NEB)

By yourself you are alone,
but with a friend you're a team
of two.

♦ Two can accomplish more than twice as much as one, for the results can be much better. If one falls, the other pulls him up; but if a man falls when he is alone, he's in trouble. Also, on a cold night, two under the same blanket gain warmth from each other, but how can one be warm alone? And one standing alone can be attacked and defeated, but two can stand back-to-back and conquer; three is even better, for a triple-braided cord is not easily broken.
ECCLESIASTES 4:9-12 (TLB)

When visiting away from home, eat what you're fed, sleep where you're put, and always say "Thank you."

Evida Biehl (my mother)

♦ These were the twelve whom Jesus sent out, with the instructions: "Don't turn off into any of the heathen roads, and don't go into any Samaritan town. Go rather to the lost sheep of the house of Israel. ... Give, as you have received, without any charge whatever. Don't take any gold or silver or even coppers to put in your purse; nor a knapsack for the journey, nor even a second coat, nor sandals nor staff—the workman deserves his keep! Wherever you go, whether it is into a town or a village, find out someone who is respected and stay with him until you leave. As you enter his house give it your blessing. If the house deserves it, the peace of your blessing will come to it. But if it doesn't, your peace will return to you." MATTHEW 10:5, 6, 8-13 (PHILLIPS)

We all learn most from friends, not enemies. If you want to convince a person, first become a friend, then present your case.

♦ [At the height of Absalom's revolt], when someone told David that Ahithophel, his advisor, was backing Absalom, David prayed, "O Lord, please make Ahithophel give Absalom foolish advice!" As they reached the spot at the top of the Mount of Olives where people worshiped God, David found Hushai the Archite waiting for him with torn clothing and earth upon his head. But David told him, "If you go with me, you will only be a burden; return to Jerusalem and tell Absalom, 'I will counsel you as I did your father.' Then you can frustrate and counter Ahithophel's advice. Zadok and Abiathar, the priests, are there. Tell them the plans that are being made to capture me, and they will send their sons Ahima-az and Jonathan to find me and tell me what is going on." 2 SAMUEL 15:31-36 (TLB)

Influence a child, you influence a life. Influence a parent, you influence a family. Influence a leader, you influence a community.

♦ Train up a child in the way he should go: and when he is old, he will not depart from it. PROVERBS 22:6 (KJV)

♦ But the angel said to him, "Do not be afraid, Zacharias, for your prayer is heard; and your wife Elizabeth will bear you a son, and you shall call his name John. And you will have joy and gladness, and many will rejoice at his birth. For he will be great in the sight of the Lord, and shall drink neither wine nor strong drink. He will also be filled with the Holy Spirit, even from his mother's womb. And he will turn many of the children of Israel to the Lord their God. He will also go before Him in the spirit and power of Elijah, 'to turn the hearts of the fathers to the children,' and the disobedient to the wisdom of the just, to make ready a people prepared for the Lord." LUKE 1:13-17 (NKJV)

A wise person considers the effects of a decision on all involved, not just himself.

♦ This is what you were called to do, because Christ suffered for you and gave you an example to follow. So you should do as he did. 1 PETER 2:21 (NCV)

The poor can act as our guides through the eye of the needle. When we help them, we find self-fulfillment and the wisdom that leads to the joys of the kingdom of God.

George Caywood

♦ And you shall not glean your vineyard, nor shall you gather every grape of your vineyard; you shall leave them for the poor and the stranger: I am the Lord your God. LEVITICUS 19:10 (NKJV)

♦ There will always be poor people in the land. Therefore I command you to be openhanded toward your brothers and toward the poor and needy in your land. DEUTERONOMY 15:11 (NIV)

♦ Good people are concerned about justice for the poor, but the wicked are not concerned. PROVERBS 29:7 (NCV)

♦ Looking at his disciples, he said: "Blessed are you who are poor, for yours is the kingdom of God." LUKE 6:20 (NIV)

Remember people's names.

♦ Greet Priscilla and Aquila, my fellow workers in Christ Jesus. They risked their lives for me. Not only I but all the churches of the Gentiles are grateful to them....

Greet my dear friend Epenetus, who was the first convert to Christ in the province of Asia.

Greet Mary, who worked very hard for you.

Greet Andronicus and Junias, my relatives....

Greet Ampliatus, whom I love in the Lord.

Greet Urbanus, our fellow worker in Christ, and my dear friend Stachys.

Greet Apelles, tested and approved in Christ....

Greet Herodion, my relative....

Greet Tryphena and Tryphosa, those women who work hard in the Lord.

Greet my dear friend Persis....

Greet Rufus, chosen in the Lord, and his mother, who has been a mother to me, too.

Greet Asyncritus, Phlegon, Hermes, Patrobas, Hermas and the brothers with them....

Greet one another with a holy kiss. ROMANS 16: 3-16 (NIV)

SPIRITUAL PRINCIPLES

Before you trust a person or
his message, study his life.

◆ For the words that the mouth utters come from the overflowing of the heart. A good man produces good from the store of good within himself; and an evil man from evil within produces evil. MATTHEW 12:35 (NEB)

◆ Anyone who listens to the word but does not do what it says is like a man who looks at his face in a mirror and, after looking at himself, goes away and immediately forgets what he looks like. But the man who looks intently into the perfect law that gives freedom, and continues to do this, not forgetting what he has heard, but doing it—he will be blessed in what he does. JAMES 1:23-25 (NIV)

God's Word, the Bible, is the world's only completely trustworthy measuring stick for truth. Without the Bible there is no absolute standard for right or wrong.

♦ All Scripture is given by inspiration of God, and is profitable for doctrine, for reproof, for correction, for instruction in righteousness, that the man of God may be complete, thoroughly equipped for every good work. 2 TIMOTHY 3:16, 17 (NKJV)

♦ For the word of God is living and active. Sharper than any double-edged sword, it penetrates even to dividing soul and spirit, joints and marrow; it judges the thoughts and attitudes of the heart. HEBREWS 4:12 (NIV)

When God seems far away, focus on biblical answers that cannot be questioned rather than life's questions that cannot be answered.

♦ I will meditate on Your precepts, and contemplate Your ways. I will delight myself in Your statutes; I will not forget Your word. PSALM 119:15, 16 (NKJV)

♦ Your word is a lamp to my feet and a light for my path. PSALM 119:105 (NIV)

He is no fool who gives that which he cannot keep to gain that which he cannot lose.

Jim Elliot

♦ For whoever desires to save his life will lose it, but whoever loses his life for My sake will save it. For what advantage is it to a man if he gains the whole world, and is himself destroyed or lost? LUKE 9:24, 25 (NKJV)

Ultimately we do everything for one of two reasons: to serve ourselves or to serve God.

♦ No one can serve two masters. Either he will hate the one and love the other, or he will be devoted to the one and despise the other. MATTHEW 6:24 (NIV)

God's timing is perfect.

♦ But when the time had fully come, God sent his Son, born of a woman, born under the law.… GALATIANS 4:4 (NIV)

Giving to God and others is like the farmer planting seed. The more he plants, the greater his harvest.

Rich Buhler

♦ Cast your bread upon the waters, for you will find it after many days. ECCLESIASTES 11:1 (NKJV)

♦ Give, and it will be given to you: good measure, pressed down, shaken together, and running over will be put into your bosom. For with the same measure that you use, it will be measured back to you. LUKE 6:38 (NKJV)

Be an absorber of pressure, not a reflector of it.

♦ A soft answer turns away wrath, but harsh words cause quarrels.
PROVERBS 15:1 (TLB)

Life is tough. Trust God and keep on keeping on.

◆ Trust in the Lord with all your heart, and lean not on your own understanding; In all your ways acknowledge Him, and He shall direct your paths. PROVERBS 3:5, 6 (NKJV)

◆ I know whom I have believed, and am persuaded that he is able to keep that which I have committed unto him against that day. 2 TIMOTHY 1:12 (KJV)

Additional Bobb Biehl Resources are available from:
>Masterplanning Group International
>Box 952499
>Lake Mary, Florida 32795

Ask for Masterplanning Group's resource catalogue, and consulting and speaking information.

>Executive Offices: 407-330-2028
>Fax: 407-330-4134
>To order materials: 800-443-1976